CW00506232

"I AM"
Affirmations

And the Secret of their Effective Use

By
Peter Mt. Shasta

Published by Church of the Seven Rays
Post Office Box 1103
Mount Shasta, California 96067

Copyright © 2012 by Peter Mt. Shasta

No part of this book may be reproduced, stored in a retrieval system, or transmitted by any means without the written permission of the author. Request for such permission should be addressed to the publisher.

First eBook edition by Smashwords June, 2012
First paperback edition August, 2012

ISBN: 978-0982807354 (Lightning Source, 2nd Edition)
ISBN: 978-1478218302 (Create Space)
ISBN: 978-0982807347 (Smashwords eBook)

Other books by Peter Mt. Shasta:
"I AM" the Open Door
Adventures of a Western Mystic: Apprentice to the Masters

Cover and book design by: Tracy Tuttle

Dedication

This book is dedicated to all those who, over the years, have requested I write down these affirmations which I previously gave during retreats.

Note of Gratitude

Many thanks to Karen Carty, Aloha Heart, Carl Marsak, Linda Jo Martin, Runa Gupta and Deepti and Miles Wilkinson for their kind assistance in the publication of this book. May the blessings generated by its publication return to you a thousand fold.

The I AM Presence

The I AM Presence is God—your Higher Self—a focus of Consciousness surrounded by the rainbow of the causal body. These colors are the positive qualities accumulated through many lifetimes of experience. Emanating from this God Self is the luminous body of the Christ Self, the intermediary between the God and human self. Some artists also show the Higher Mental Body or Soul existing in a yet lower dimension.

A tube of conscious energy is projected downward from the heart of the God Self through the various dimensions until it is anchored in the human body near the thymus gland in the center of the chest. This is often perceptible as the flame or energy focus which sustains and gives us guidance, portrayed artistically as the Fleur de Lis, the three fold flame of Love, Wisdom and Power. Awareness of this flame is the key to conscious Mastery.

The lifestream completes its earthly journey only when the consciousness of the human and God Self are united within the heart, and we become a living Christ.

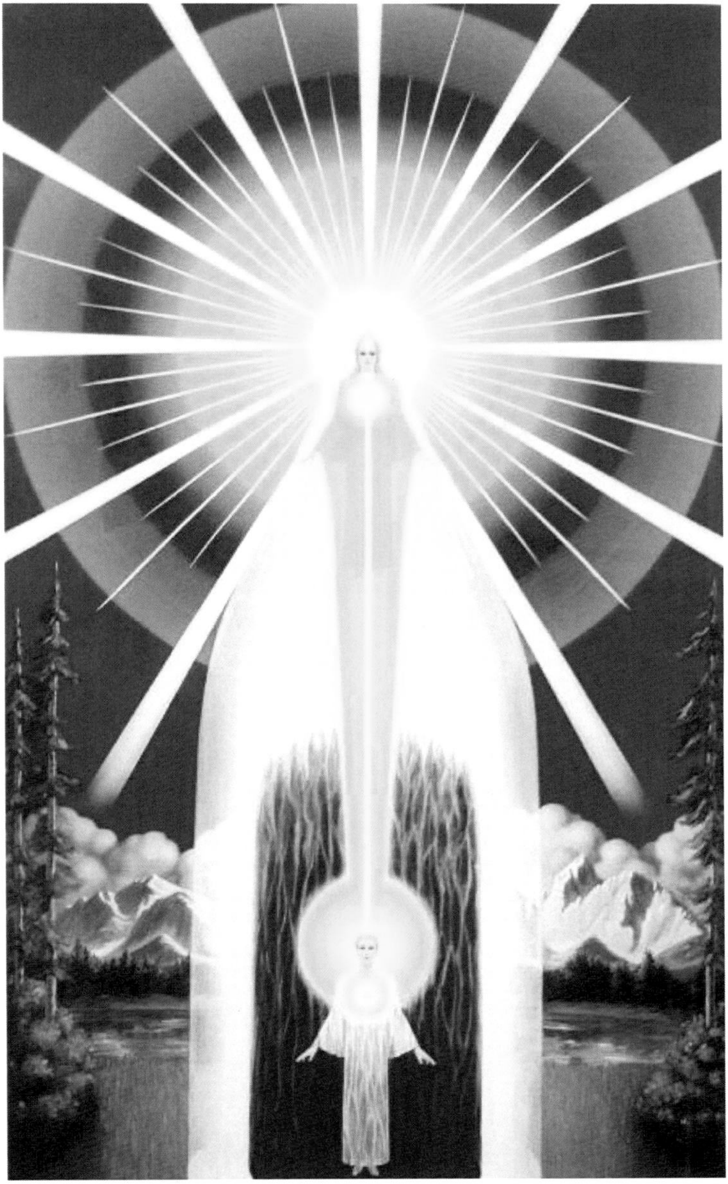

The I AM Presence

CONTENTS

Before Abraham, was I AM.
-John 8:58

And God said unto Moses, I AM THAT I AM.
-Exodus 3:13-14

In the beginning was the Word, and the Word was with God, and the Word was God.
-John 1:1

I AM the beginning, the middle and the end of all creation... I AM the origin of all being... There is nothing, animate or inanimate, that can exist without Me.
-Lord Krishna, "Bhagavad-Gita"

The Great "I AM"

The use of Affirmations is an ancient yet powerful way to influence reality. However, one must first realize that the doorway to the reality to be changed is within oneself. What you can change is within you. To try to influence something "out there" with ego, mind and willpower only creates a karmic link binding one to the consequences of that forceful action.

Once you realize the true nature of reality within yourself, you see things in a new light, that for the lessons we need to learn things may already be the way they are supposed to be, and without any need for intervention. Perhaps the change that is required is within our own perceptions? Regardless, inward change is the only way effective change is achieved anywhere, for all outer change begins within.

From the beginning of time "I AM" has been known as the secret name of God. Since we are made "in the image and likeness of God," it is also our secret name, and in knowing how to tap into that true essence we become creators capable of miracles. Using "I AM" affirmations we can guide our consciousness to bring forth whatever the Universe wishes into form and manifestation. This process is so simple even a child can accomplish it, for all that is needed is the belief that whatever can be conceived of is possible.

However, we must first realize that as our divine nature has duplicated itself in human form, that "I" has also created its own shadow, the ego, which tries to usurp our consciousness by pretending it is the source, center and goal of our world. Only when we see that dual nature, the illusory self and the true self that is the Source of our being, can we progress on the path of mastery and conscious creation.

Otherwise we are merely replicating our own confusion in the world, and assuring that we will have to come back to experience the consequences of our misdirected thoughts and actions—and every thought is an action.

To see this more clearly, imagine you are sitting in a movie theatre. You are watching an exciting film filled with action, romance and adventure. It is so well written, acted and directed that you find yourself drawn into the story. You forget you are in a theatre, and become the living drama. However, the story does not go as you like. It becomes so painful you take a deep breath and look around for escape. Then you realize that you are only in a theatre, watching an imaginary story. You look backward at the light from the projector shining over your head, and you breathe a sigh of relief, for you realize that you have only been watching digital images of light animated on the screen before you. You remember who you are, that you are not part of that drama, that you are a separate individual who was drawn into something not real by the seduction of your attention.

By remaining in touch with the breath, the rising and falling of your chest, and by being aware of the light in the area of your heart where your soul is anchored, you can simultaneously observe the movie and learn the lesson it holds for you, yet at the same time remain aware that you are not that. You are the living light, the light that gives life and illuminates reality wherever your attention flows.

You have awakened to the realization that you are not that story. But what about your story? What about the drama of your own life, your own movie? Have you awakened to that illusion? Can you observe that film, knowing that you are not that, that your daily life is merely a series of thoughts, feelings and images made relatively real by the light of your own inner light? When you have realized your true nature then you can create consciously without creating the negative residue called karma.

This is where meditation comes in. "Meditation" means going to the middle, the center of your being, where you look into that light and see revealed about you the shadows you had thought were real, which you can now dissolve. There, in the center of your being, you realize your true, unlimited nature.

You see the two "I"s, the ego identified with the dream body, acting more or less selfishly and unconsciously in your movie, playing the part assigned it as a result of past life actions; and you see the other "I," the free, unlimited light that is the Consciousness of your True Self.

The miracle of this paradox is that one does not necessarily exclude the other. You can be aware of the True Self, the absolute "I," and still play your part in the movie of your life, the egoic role of the relative "I," much as an actor wears a costume. In being thus conscious you are in the world but not of the world. You are an ordinary being among other ordinary beings, except that you are conscious of who you are, and no longer motivated by ignorance, doubt, and selfishness. When you are aware of your True Self you see that those negative qualities of the illusory self only lead to bondage, limitation and suffering, while identifying with your True Self leads to wisdom, compassion, bliss and enlightened action.

Gradually, as you keep returning your focus to the center of your being, the illusion of the lower self dissolves, and there is only one "I." There is only one unbroken stream of consciousness. Just as you can have a conversation with someone and at the same time hear the wind in the trees and see a cloud passing over the face of the sun, so too can you be aware of your unlimited and limited natures. Once in this consciousness you are on the path of self mastery, and can do the work of a Bodhisattva in compassionate service to others.

The Secret of Affirmations

To be effective as masters we must cut through the illusion of a separate self identified with ego, and return to the consciousness of the Source, the I AM THAT I AM, the God Self. In that Oneness there is no separation between thought and reality, between energy and matter. You are one with all, and all is a part of you. Hence, your thoughts manifest instantaneously. The only obstacle to that manifestation is habitual identification with limitation and prior agreements you may have made before birth to experience the illusion of limitation in various situations in order to learn certain lessons.

The purpose of this book is to give simple yet powerful instruction that will enable you to realize the purpose of your being, and break the habitual identification with the lower self, and through meditating on powerful affirmations make the transition to being the higher self in thought, word and deed.

What you put your attention on, you become. As you think and feel, so it is. Where your treasure is there your heart is, and there you are. This Law of Attention is the eternal Law of Creation by which all that is was brought into being; the same law by which all that is yet to be will be created. By this law you too can create.

The moment you think, you have brought a form into being; and the more you think on, feel and love that form which you have visualized the more real it becomes. Eventually the thought form precipitates in the human world. This is how the Masters create, and how you create, even if unconsciously.

As the Bible says in John 1, "In the beginning was the Word, and the Word was with God, and the Word was God," so it is through speaking that Word, thinking and feeling that Word, that all is created; and That Word is I AM. With that phrase you invoke your own God Self, right here and now.

This is the secret of affirmations. What you think with your mind, what you feel with your heart and what you say with your words you bring forth into the world. The key, however, is to speak with Love. Think or say the affirmations with love, for love is the mother which nurtures your intentions and brings them to birth. It is out of that love, the substance found in the great Inner Silence, from which all comes into being.

This means that what you wish to create, what you wish to be, must come from a place of surrender to the Divine, the Higher Self, not from an assertion of the ego, the "me," the personality of the lower self that has countless desires to create what it wants. Anything created from that self only leads to materialism and bondage. To create happiness and freedom, every act must come from and be a surrender to the Higher Self, the Great I AM. Only here should an affirmation originate and be allowed to flow forth into being. In this way every act is the creative

Divine Will flowing through you—which you affirm and bring into being with your words. This is the Word of God in Action—the Divine Law which must manifest.

In order to reach this place of surrender the ego, mind, emotions and personality must be stilled and made servant to the Higher Self, the Great I AM. This is accomplished through meditation. One of the simplest and most effective forms of meditation is to visualize and feel a light in the center of your chest, and feel the love and warmth of that light expanding like the rays of an inner sun. Then, emanating from the center of that sun comes the great command, "I AM," from which all affirmations, all acts of creation flow.

To still the lower self you can use the simple meditation of observing the breath that Buddha used to become enlightened. It is powerful and effective, yet so simple that any child can use it with little practice. Simply feel the process of your breathing. Focus your attention on that sensation of the rise and fall of your chest as the breath goes naturally in and out. Do not control the breath; simply observe the in-breath and the out-breath. When your mind wanders, label it "thinking," and come back to the rise and fall of your chest. Keep your eyes slightly open, gazing at the floor, spine straight, and tongue against the roof of the mouth to complete the circuit of bio-electric energy through the subtle nervous system. Hands can rest in the Buddha pose, palms up, the back of one hand resting in the palm of the other, thumbs almost touching. Or, you can sit with your palms on your knees, thumb and index finger touching.

The important thing is your attention. The breath is like a mantra that can not be forgotten, for it is with you throughout life from the moment of birth, a mantra which you can now use for enlightenment. This is the simplest meditation on earth, yet difficult to do with one-pointed attention, for that little stray puppy of the mind wants to go its own way, to run here and there. Yet that little puppy, without training in obedience, will grow up into a big dog that will run your life from morning 'til night. You must show it who is master; keep pulling on the leash of your attention, without anger or frustration—just the simple reminder: Pay attention to the breath, the doorway to conscious self-awareness.

If you find this difficult, try counting your out-breaths up to ten, and then count back down from ten to one. Then repeat the process. If your mind wanders label those thoughts or sensations "thinking," and bring your attention back to the sequence. Soon you will become aware of an expanded consciousness, the realization of awareness itself, as you loosen the hold your mind has had over you. You become master of your mind, ruler of your attention—and the door to conscious creation is open.

Once you have stilled the mind, the second step is to feel the creative God Flame in the center of your being. It is not in the physical heart, but the flame of your Soul slightly to the right of the sternum. You can feel it as a warm, golden light, an emanation of love. With your attention on that center of life, you feel it throb and expand. This is the energy that has been trying to guide you throughout your life, trying to point you always in the right direction. Now you can follow it more consciously and head its promptings. This Presence, which is both Light and Love, can be expanded without limit, guided by your conscious intention.

This "I" is the two-fold activity of the father-fire-electronic-will aspect, and the "AM" is the activity of the mother-earth-magnetic-love aspect, both of which must function together to manifest the full creative power of the I AM activity. This electronic-magnetic duality is the force that powers the universe, that holds planets and electrons in their orbits. Similarly, an electric motor works because of a flow of electrons through a wire as well as the magnetic field surrounding that wire. Only with both qualities of consciousness functioning together does the rotor spin.

The feeling side of human nature is the feminine activity of consciousness within every individual. The thought is the masculine activity of the mind. A thought never becomes dynamic in the outer life until it passes through the feeling body. The feeling condenses upon the thought pattern, the atomic substance of the outer activity of life. In thus passing through the feeling body, the thought becomes clothed, and thereafter exists as a separate living thing outside of the individual's mind.
-Godfre Ray King, "The Magic Presence"

You also are a great engine of consciousness which can employ both the positive and negative polarity of God's Force to bring anything into manifestation. Just the mind or the will working alone only generates resistance; and love without will, vision, and direction remains inert. But, when will and love unite you create miracles; and it is this union of love and will that powers affirmations and brings forth creation.

Increasing the volume and speed of affirmations is usually counterproductive, for ego's will blocks the flow of love from the heart, actually creating the opposite effect. Acts of creation come from the stillness of surrender to the Divine, as in the stillness of the mother's womb. It is there in the Silence that creativity becomes empowered with the love that is the source of all creative acts. It is neither the "I" nor the "AM" alone, but the "I AM" flowing together that brings things into manifestation.

Before you start affirming what you want ask your great God Presence within and above you what It wants."

> *Dear God, show me what you want.*
> *Thy will, not my will, be done.*

Here the secret of affirmation begins, in surrender before the God Presence. After you have stilled the mind, connected with the love of your Divine Self and placed yourself in service to that Presence, then your affirmations will be effective—for you will be affirming what your God Self truly desires, not merely trying to acquire what the ego wants.

Use affirmations to say "Yes" to life, to what God wants to come forth, and your acceptance will make that a reality. When you align your will with Divine Will every affirmation manifests results instantaneously. Remember, though, not to judge the effect of your affirmations with the limited eyes of ego, which wants to see everything manifest on the material plane immediately. Just like the seed planted in soil that needs time to germinate and sprout, so too affirmations sometimes need time to manifest all their attributes in visible form. Be patient, and know your affirmation is working. All words spoken with intent and love manifest immediately, sending out vibrations and energy into the universe. How and when visible, tangible results manifest in your three dimensional world is up to God.

Let go of all attachment to the results, just as once the seed is planted in the garden you must leave it alone, undisturbed. To pull up the seed and examine how it is doing will only delay or stop it's growth entirely. That is the hard part, to set something in motion and then get out of the way, waiting to see how the God Consciousness acts and creates in its own way and time. Know that God's intention will manifest according to the plan for our highest evolution.

To Amplify an Affirmation

Make sure that your meditation has four parts:

1) Verbal

2) Visualization

3) Feeling

4) Action.

Use these four parts together to manifest results.

With some affirmations you may use a hand gesture (mudra) as the action. This can be simply opening the palms of the hands to receive what you are invoking, such as abundance, or placing a hand on the part of the body you wish to perfect. The slightest gesture, if done consciously, can produce a profound results.

An affirmation only needs to be said once if done in full consciousness. However, to be sure of being fully effective they may be repeated three or even seven times. Additionally, one may invoke the Masters, "I call on the Ascended Host of Light to come forth and amplify this affirmation for the Highest Good, by the Power of the Three Times Three which I AM."

Jesus
Photograph reported to have appeared on the film of Ana Ali,
a nun from Kenya, while visiting Rome on September 8, 1987.

Affirmations for Spiritual Realization

S-1.   **I AM the Presence of God.**

S-2.   **I AM the Living Light.**

S-3.   **I AM the Light of the world.**

S-4.   **I AM Love.**

S-5.   **I AM the Sun of God.**
         *Extended your arms to each side, visualizing light
         radiating from your palms.*

S-6.   **I AM the Living Christ.**
         Extend your arms in blessing

S-7.   **I AM One with All.**

S-8.   **I AM my Divine Conscious now come through.**

S-9.   **I AM the Consciousness that I had in God
         before the beginning of the world.**

S-10.   **I AM the Love, Wisdom and Power of God in
         action.**

S-11.   I AM the Master Presence, God in physical form.

S-12.   I AM Faith, Hope, Charity, Compassion, Wisdom, Understanding (or any other quality) now made fully manifest in my life and world.

S-13.   I AM the Alpha and the Omega, the beginning and the end, the first and the last, the One Eternal Presence of all that is.

S-14.   I AM the Great Divine Director of my life and world.

S-15.   I AM Holy, Pure and Perfect.

S-16.   I AM here, I AM there, I AM the only Presence acting everywhere.

S-17.   I AM the Resurrection and the Life.

S-18.   I AM the Ascension in the Light.

S-19.   I AM the Luminous Presence of Jesus.

S-20 . I AM a White Fire Being from the heart of the Great Central Sun.

S-21.   I AM Love, Love, Love.

S-22.   I AM Light, Light, Light.

S-23.   I AM God, God, God.

S-24.   **I AM that I AM THAT I AM.**

My own Affirmations:

Affirmations for
God Dominion and Protection

D-1.   I AM the Commanding, Governing Presence going before me throughout this day, commanding perfect Peace, Love, Wisdom, Harmony and the Ascended Masters Perfect Divine Plan in all activity.

D-2.   Serenely I fold my wings and abide in the wisdom of my Presence, untouched by outer, human creation.

D-3.   I stand One With God, above all human creation.

D-4.   I AM Invincibly Protected.

D-5.   I AM my Invincible Tube of Light now made fully manifest about me, and forever fully self sustained.

D-6.   I AM the Crystal Cloak of Mighty Victory.

D-7.   I AM come forth and take complete command here!

D-8. In the name of the Love, Wisdom and Power of the Presence of God that I AM, I say to all human creation, You have no power over me.

D-9. I AM the Great White Brotherhood in action here.

D-10. The Light of God Never Fails! The Light of God Never Fails! The Light of God Never Fails, and I AM That Light!

D-11. I AM God in action here.

D-12. I AM the Master Presence in action here.

D-13. I AM the Presence of God dissolving and consuming anything less than perfection.

D-14. I AM the Miracle Working Presence taking complete command of this situation, and bringing about the Perfect Divine Plan here (there).

D-15. I AM the Conscious Activity and Directing Power of the Cosmic Christ.

D-16. I AM Ascended Master Friends and the Ascended Masters themselves, raised up before and about me, bringing about the Perfect Divine Plan in all activity.

D-17. I AM the Open Door, which no man can shut.

D-18.　I AM the Living Light going before me.

D-19.　I AM the Invincible Guard fully established, sustained and maintained about this car, house, building, land, activity (etc.) at all times, by the Full Power, Activity and Dominion of God forever.

D-20.　I AM the Presence of Mighty Prince Astrea clearing all psychic influence from this place (person or situation).
This Master clears the astral realm, which is composed of human thoughts and emotions, and frees individuals from its psychic pressure. The realms of spirit are above the astral, and should be called the "etheric".

D-21.　I AM the Invincible Guard fully established, sustained and maintained about my home and property at all times from hence forth.

D-22.　I AM Protected by the Great White Brotherhood now and at all times.

My own Affirmations:

Affirmations for Guidance

G-1.   I AM going where I AM meant to go, doing what I AM meant to do.

G-2.   I AM the Illumining, Revealing Presence showing me the Divine Plan here (for this activity).

G-3.   I AM the I AM Presence and the Ascended Host of Light, dissolving and consuming anything that might interfere with my guidance, and setting me on the right path now this instant. See to it that I do what I AM meant to do, and I AM doing it.

G-4.   I AM the Presence of God driving this car (flying this plane, operating this computer, machine, etc.).

G-5.   I AM Free of all desire to go anywhere I AM not meant to go, and filled with the desire and feeling to go where I AM meant to go, and I AM going there in Perfect Divine Order.

G-6.   I AM seeing the Divine Plan now for this situation, and doing my part perfectly.

G-7.   I AM the Great White Brotherhood guiding me this instant, opening all doors, and clearing all obstacles from my path by the Power of God that I AM.

My own Affirmations:

Affirmations for Abundance

A-1.   I AM the Abundance of God.

A-2.   I AM the Wealth of God now made manifest in my hands and use, and which I AM using perfectly to fulfill God's Divine Plan.

A-3.   I AM the Limitless Wealth of Creation now come forth for all the people of the earth.

A-4.   I AM the Great Divine Director of my business and finances.

A-5.   I AM Ascended Master Friends raised up before and about me, helping me with all my business and financial dealings, seeing to it that I act under Divine Direction for the greatest good always.

A-6.   I AM employed by the Great White Brotherhood for the benefit of humanity, and am supported in that work Perfectly and in Complete Abundance.

A-7.   I AM being shown how to generate abundant cash flow right here and now, and I AM doing it.

A-8.   I AM the Illumining, Revealing Presence, showing me the truth of all financial dealings, offers & contracts, protecting me from making any wrong decisions, and seeing to it that I only make agreements under Divine Guidance.

A-9.   I AM being stopped from signing any contract or making any agreement that is not according to Plan.

A-10.   I AM the instantaneous precipitation and manifestation of all the money I require now made manifest in my hands and bank account.

A-11.   I AM the Presence bringing into instantaneous manifestation the situation, goods and resources I require.

My own Affirmations:

Affirmations for Health

H-1.   I AM my Perfect Health now made fully manifest.

H-2.   I AM the Perfect Harmony of my mind, body and feelings.

H-3.   I AM the Resurrection and the Life of every cell of my body.

H-4.   I AM the Living Light flowing through every cell, organ, nerve, bone and tissue of my body, establishing all in perfect health, function and well being.

Draw your hands down over your head, face, arms, torso, legs, feet, and to your toes, saying to yourself, "This is the perfect body of God."

H-5.   I AM flooding my cells with the Harmonious Light of God.

H-6.   I AM my Perfect Health now and forever fully self sustained.

H-7.   I AM Holy, Pure and Perfect.

H-8.   I AM the Great Divine Director of my diet, showing me what to eat and seeing to it that I do so.

H-9.   I AM free of all desire for anything I should not eat, and filled only with the desire to eat and drink what is healthy for me.

H-10.   I AM being guided to the perfect foods, supplements and substances that will establish, sustain and maintain me in perfect health and vitality at all times.

H-11.   I AM invincibly protected from any substance that might be harmful for me.

H-12.   I AM the Resurrection and the Life of my cells (or any organ or system).

H-13.   I AM being guided to the perfect physician or health practitioner to assist me in my healing.

H-14.   I AM God in action in this physician (practitioner or hospital) seeing to it that they do the perfect thing for me.

H-15.   I AM the Great White Brotherhood taking complete command of my health so that I may be of assistance in God's Divine Plan.

H-16.   I AM invincibly protected from all that is less than perfection.

H-17.   **I AM the Healing Presence of God, healing all who contact me, see me, say my name, or even think of me.**

H-18.   **I AM the Medicine Buddha in action, radiating healing wherever it is needed.**

H-19.   **I AM the Healing Christ in action, healing all who come to me.**

H-20.   **I AM the Resurrection and the Life of my Digestion.**

Hold the left hand out to your side, palm up, visualizing a ray of light from the I AM Presence coming down into it. The energy flows through your body to your right hand, which you place on your abdomen and rotate in a clockwise direction nine times [clockwise to someone facing you]. Feel the healing energy.

My own Affirmations:

Affirmations For Relationships

R-1.　　I AM seeing God in everyone at all times.

R-2.　　I AM kept away from those with whom I AM not meant to be.

R-3.　　I AM revealing the purpose of this connection, and seeing to it that I do only what is right and according to the Divine Plan.

R-4.　　I AM invincibly protected from any relationship or association that is not under Divine Direction.

R-5.　　I AM God's Love flowing forth to you.

R-6.　　I AM the Love, Wisdom and Guidance of God in our relationship.

R-7.　　I AM the Presence of God, and you are the Presence of God, and we are the Presence of God together in Love and Harmony.

Visualize your partner as a Deity (Master) who has come into your life to teach, bless and nurture you.

R-8.　　I AM being shown how to improve our relationship.

R-9.　I AM becoming a more compassionate and loving person at all times and under all circumstances.

R-10.　I AM free of all judgment, condemnation and anger toward myself or others.

R-11.　I AM the Illumining, Revealing Presence of God showing us what we need to work on, and healing every wound and unresolved emotional issue whatever the source, making us healthy, whole and loving always.

R-12.　I AM acting toward all the way I want all to act toward me.

R-13.　I AM incapable of saying or doing anything hurtful to my partner, acting with love and compassion at all times, seeing that my partner is also myself.

R-14.　I AM true to the God Presence That I AM in this relationship, for only in the freedom of That Presence can True Love prevail.

R-15.　I AM being shown if this relationship is meant to be, and if not I call on the Ascended Host of Light to take command here and bring about the Perfect Divine Plan for each of us in Perfect Love and Harmony.

Affirmations for Parenting

PA-1. **I AM the Perfect Parent.**

PA-2. **I AM the Illumining Revealing Presence showing me everything I need to know about my child, and how to act at all times to bring about the Divine Plan for my him (her).**

PA-3. **I AM communicating with my child with love, wisdom, understanding and compassion at all times.**

PA-4. **I AM come forth! Take complete command of this situation!**

PA-5. **Beloved Ascended Masters, this is your child, so please bring about your Divine Plan for him (her).**

PA-6. **I AM the Great Divine Director of this child.**

PA-7. **I AM the Great White Brotherhood protecting my child this day, seeing that he (she) is supplied with all that is needed.**

Visualize the Masters and Angels in a circle above your child, beaming protective light down around him or her.

PA-8.   I AM being shown how parenthood is a path to my own mastery.

PA-9.   I AM clearing my issues with my own parents, so that I do not project them onto my children.

PA-10. I AM God the Mother. I AM God the Father. I AM blessing God the Child.

PA-11. I AM here, I AM there, I AM God blessing my children everywhere.

My own Affirmations:

Affirmations for the
Violet Consuming Flame

V-1.   I AM the Violet Consuming Flame in action here (or in that situation).

Violet is the most purifying and spiritually raising quality of light, and comes under the activity of the Ascended Master Saint Germain. Visualize it blazing up, in, around and through any person, place, condition or thing you wish to see purified and raised into a higher expression of life. It is also called into action by the feeling of forgiveness.

V-2.   I AM the Violet Consuming Flame blazing up, in, around and through me (or that situation), dissolving and consuming anything less than perfection, by the Power of God that I AM.

V-3.   I AM the Violet Fire of Forgiveness, dissolving and consuming all discord and untruth between_____ and me, restoring all to Perfect Divine Love, Harmony and Order.

V-4.   I AM the Presence of Saint Germain, I Am the Violet Consuming Flame. *(x3)*

V-5.   I AM the Angels of the Violet Consuming Flame come forth here (there) now.

V-6.   **I AM the Purity of Saint Germain, en-
folded in Violet Consuming Flame.**

*See yourself within a neon tube of violet light,
extending three feet on either side, reaching from
the center of the Earth and extending into the I AM
Presence above you.*

V-7.   **I AM the Presence of Saint Germain, estab-
lishing, sustaining and maintaining this lo-
cation as a focus of the Violet Consuming
Flame forever, that all who come here may
be purified.**

My own Affirmations:

Affirmations to Invoke Creativity

C-1.   I AM the Creativity of God in Action.

C-2.   I AM Inspired to bring forth whatever God wants for the benefit of others.

C-3.   I AM the Illumining, Revealing Presence showing me how to manifest God's Divine Plan for this project.

C-4.   I AM inspired right now to create the Perfect Art (Literature, Invention, etc.).

C-5.   I AM the Great White Brotherhood in action, bringing forth now what is meant to be.

C-6.   I AM being shown what to do, and I AM doing it perfectly.

C-7.   I AM One with the Mind of God, revealing what I AM meant to create.

C-8.   I AM going forth consciously in my Higher Body to the Ascended Master Retreats, where I AM working in harmony with the Masters to bring forth all that will benefit humanity.

C-9.   **I AM God in Action bringing forth what will be of benefit to humanity.**

My own Affirmations:

Affirmations for Other Purposes

O-1.   I AM going before me through this store, guided and attracted to only what I AM meant to have, and repelled by and ignoring all else.

O-2.   I AM being shown what to order from this menu and I AM ordering it, and not attracted to anything else.

O-3.   I AM the Great Divine Director of my computer, telephone and all my other electrical equipment.

O-4.   I AM the Resurrection and the Life of my car, which is maintained perfectly at all times. Every atom of my car is the Consciousness of God in action.

O-5.   I AM the Invincible Guard fully established, sustained and maintained about my computer, its operating system, programs, drives and files at all times, protecting them from all surveillance, radiation, interference or intrusion of any sort, by the Power of God which I AM. So be it, and it is done, and I thank you.

O-6.   I AM the Great Divine Director of all the governments of the Earth.

O-7.   I AM the Great Divine Director of all the military and police forces of the Earth.

O-8.   I Am the presence of Saint Germain, the Goddess of Justice and the Lords of Karma come forth through all courts, legal and administrative justice systems, bringing all into harmony with the Ascended Masters Divine Plan.

O-9.   I AM the Great Divine Director of all prisons and places of detention, freeing all who do not belong there immediately.

O-10.   I AM the Great Divine Director of the world economy and international banking system, bringing about Divine Abundance for all.

O-11.   I AM Divine Justice come forth now through every court and legal proceeding.

O-12.   I AM the Illumining Revealing Presence showing me what I need to work on within myself, and healing all wounds of which I may not even be aware.

O-13.   I AM learning from every moment in life.

O-14.   I AM growing in self mastery.

O-15. I AM the Presence taking out of me anything less
than perfection, and dissolving and consuming
it forever.

O-16. I AM dealing with myself so that others do not
have to.

My own Affirmations:

Affirmations to
Invoke Specific Masters

M-1.   **I AM the Presence of the Ascended Master Saint Germain come forth now.**

Saint Germain is the Master in charge of the new age of freedom and enlightenment. He has brought forth the ancient wisdom in the form now of the "I AM" Teachings. He also works in government, military affairs and the establishment of free society.

M-2.   **I AM the Presence of Archangel Michael.**

Archangel Michael takes discarnate, earth-bound entities off the Earth to a place where they can progress, in addition to being the wielder of the Sword of Blue Flame and commander of the Angels of Blue Lightning. Call on him only after using the Violet Consuming Flame, as his action can be dramatic and upsetting.

M-3.   **I AM the Presence of Mighty Victory.**

The being known as Victory has never known defeat. Call on him to give you courage, strength and energy to overcome any obstacle. Stand with your right hand raised, visualizing yourself as Him, a tall, golden-robed Master of golden light, grasping a sword of light.

M-4.   **I AM the Presence of Mighty Prince Astrea, clearing all psychic interference, and dissolving all astral entities from_____.**

The astral plane is the earthly accumulation of thoughts and residual emotions, also known as the realm of the psychic. Many people perceive these entities, energies and thought forms and mistake them for guidance, unlike the light that is available to the individual who is willing to work on themselves, and which comes from the I AM Presence or the Ascended Masters.

M-5.   **I AM the Goddess of Light.**

Self explanatory. Call on her when you wish more light to come forth. At one point Saint Germain said that when she dissolved the astral plane over New York City her activity generated so much light that even he could barely see her.

M-6.   **I AM Quan Yin, filled with compassion, helping wherever I AM needed.**

M-7.   **I AM Mother Mary in the Heart of the World.**

M-8.   **I AM the Presence of Lady Master Nada.**

This great being has been responsible for raising previous civilizations to their state of perfection. She was known in ancient Greece as the Goddess Athena.

M-9.   **I AM Faith, Hope and Charity.**

Originally charity did not mean giving to the poor, but the quality of loving compassion, or unconditional love. Faith does not mean blind faith, but is generated by the certainty of knowing the truth. Hope is not passive, but the strength of aspiration to attain a certain accomplishment.

M-10.   **I AM the Presence of Grace.**

In ancient Greece the traditional feminine qualities embodied in enlightened society were personified by the Three Graces long portrayed by artists, although they are more numerous and include: Grace, Splendor, Mirth, Festivity, Cheer and others. Life would be dull without them, so their qualities should be invoked and cultivated.

M-11.   **I AM the Presence of the Gods of the Mountains: Himalaya, Meru, Tabor and the God of the Swiss Alps.**

Every great mountain is a focus of spiritual consciousness that blesses the surroundings and helps stabilize the earth. These are four of the best known of those Deities.

M-12.   **I AM the Presence of Master Leto teaching me to travel consciously in my etheric body.**

This lady master plays an extensive role in the Magic Presence, by Godfre Ray King, and her presence is often accompanied by the scent of heather.

M-13.   **I AM the Pearl of Great Price.**

Invoke Lady Master Pearl, who serves under Saint Germain and helps all, but especially the ladies, attune to the I AM Presence within. The pearl is symbolic of the process of enfolding one's pain with love to produce wisdom and compassion.

M-14.   **I AM the Presence of the Archangels.**

Although little is known about them other than that they are great beings aligned with the will of God, they can be invoked as a group to give a great blessing to an area or activity. Or, they can be invoked separately. The names of the most well known Archangels are: Michael, Gabriel, Raphael, Chamuel, Uriel, Jophiel, Zadkiel and Metatron.

M-15.   **I AM the Presence of the Angelic Host of Light: the Seraphim, Cherubim, Thrones, Dominions, Principalities, Powers, Virtues, Archangels and Angels, bringing Harmony and Perfection to all Creation.**

These are Messengers of God, or may be thought of as aspects of Universal Consciousness, who carry out the functions of maintaining the order of the Cosmos, such as keeping the planets in their orbit, recording the history of time, guiding the development of consciousness, etc.

M-16.   **I AM blessing and giving gratitude to the Elementals.**

These are the nature spirits of the four elements: fire, air, earth and water, without whom life on earth would not be possible. They nurture and bring forth all life, and appreciate and benefit from our gratitude.

My Own Affirmations

My Own Affirmations

My Own Affirmations

Warning:
Using an affirmation to influence another person or situation for selfish purposes will in the long run produce an undesired effect, for thoughts and energy travel in a circle, returning to the sender greatly amplified. What you are experiencing now is what you created in past lives. Hence, only use affirmations to create what you want to experience in the future.

Saint Germain is the Ascended Master responsible for bringing in the dawning age of freedom in which all know their Source, the I AM Presence. His last human embodiment was as Sir Francis Bacon, the legitimate (yet secret) son of Queen Elizabeth and the Earl of Leister, and rightful heir to the throne of England. He was the true author of the Shakespeare plays and the final editor of the King James Bible. When he could no longer be of service due to the intrigues of the court, he staged a mock funeral and escaped to Europe where, using the name Christian Rosencreuz, he founded the mystical Rosicrucian Order. Subsequently he journeyed to Tibet, where he completed his ascension.

In later years he began appearing in the courts of Europe in his Ascended Master body, using various disguises in which he worked toward establishing an era of peace, enlightenment and brotherhood. Many accounts of his activity leading up to the French Revolution appear in the diaries of various ladies of the court. These journals are now held in the British Library, and are quoted extensively in The Count of Saint Germain *by Isabel Cooper-Oakley.*

He was also instrumental in the founding of the United States of America, as described in Manley P. Halls, The Secret Destiny of America. *The I AM teachings, which contain the secret wisdom of the ages, are his gift to the world.*

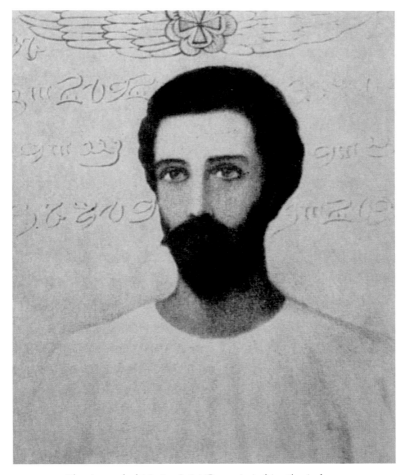

The Ascended Master Saint Germain in his etheric form.

Peter Mt. Shasta, 2010

BOOKS BY THE SAME AUTHOR:

"I AM" the Open Door

Also in eBook and translated into several foreign languages. Teachings on realizing and bringing the I AM Presence into daily life, given directly by various Ascended Masters, some in female form, who often appeared visibly during the transmission.

Adventures of a Western Mystic: Apprentice to the Masters

Also in eBook. Autobiographical experiences of the author's meetings with the Ascended Masters, sometimes in physical form, and his attempts to apply the I AM teachings which they gave him.

"I AM" Affirmations
And the Secret of their Effective Use
By Peter Mt. Shasta

"An instant classic in the field of applied spirituality."
-S.G, Portland, Oregon

"This book has helped me understand better how to apply affirmations. It has brought clarity to how affirmations work. I am able connect to the affirmations, giving them more inner power. I love that affirmations have been listed for different scenarios. It's an easy read. Highly recommend it."
–R.G., San Diego, California

Lightning Source UK Ltd.
Milton Keynes UK
UKRC02n1434140617
303298UK00001B/11